The Obvious:
Universal Laws for Business Success

Bill Walsh

Books may be purchased for educational, business or sales promotional use.
For more information please contact:
Special Promotions Department, Caboodle Publishing, P.O. Box 460303,
Centennial, CO 80046 or visit www.caboodlepublishing.com

FIRST EDITION
Published by Caboodle Publishing – Denver, CO

Library of Congress Cataloging-in-Publication Data
ISBN: 978-0-9788799-5-2
ISBN-10:   0-9788799-5-3
10 9 8 7 6 5 4 3 2 1

More Praise for Bill Walsh and *The Obvious*

"Bill gives us years of treasured experiences distilled into his 'best of the best' formula to achieve our dreams and greater success! He reminds us of easy to understand steps that most know yet few are willing to consistently apply. His heartfelt inspirational speaking comes through in a style that allows the reader to learn and more importantly apply what Bill has shared with millions already through Powerteam International. Buy it, read it, and use it, and become a better you!"
Dr. Rich Schuttler, International public speaker, educator, and author

 "In business it is often the most obvious things that can easily be overlooked which leads to a detrimental impact on the success of a company. Bill has identified these obvious universal laws that will help any business owner increase performance, revenues and market share. It takes more than motivation to make it in this world; it takes application of proven tools which Bill gives you. Read, study and take action for results!"
Sheila Stewart, Executive Business Coach, International Speaker and Bestselling Author of *Backwards in High Heels – a Woman's Guide to Succeeding in Business* and *99 Killer Business Ideas*

"The Obvious is the real deal, none of the hype and promise of riches. It shows you how to apply every day principles to get what you want out of your life. There is no secret, only The Obvious."
Austin Walsh, International Speaker and Social Media Expert

Dedication

Dedicated to your Success!

Acknowledgments

Thank you to all the supporters and contributors to what has made Powerteam International and our programs possible.

I would like to thank my Mother and Father for believing in the impossible!

I would especially like to thank my kids Austin, Marissa and Evan

For being the best kids a Dad could ever wish for!

I would also like to thank all of the amazing customers that we have at Powerteam International for making the journey possible!

Together, we will live the dream!

Foreword

Are you ready for a breakthrough? I highly recommend *The Obvious*. This book will change your life. Why call it *The Obvious*? Well, it's common sense, but not common practice. Think about that. This book will change your life. It's a tool that I use right now, that my children use, my friends use, and my colleagues use. It's changing lives...and it will change yours, too!

It's changing my life. It's expanding my world. I realize that you're never too old to learn; and you're never too young to teach. And let me share something with you, Bill Walsh has done himself proud. He's done really well. This will change your life. You will never be the same again.

Well, what is it? It's *The Obvious*—yes, it is. I mean, when you think about it, it's there already. You just don't see it until your eyes are unlensed...and you say, "Whoa! It's been there all the time."

There are two main reasons I recommend *The Obvious*:

No. 1 – In today's world, things have changed; and that means you've got to change.

No. 2 – In today's world, you need to develop a new skill set.

The Obvious will help you develop a new mindset in order to make it today. You see, if you look at yourself and look around you, you'll see ordinary people are doing what they feel they need to do.

Here's what *The Obvious* will do for you: It will empower you with the knowledge and the content to do what you are called to do. Once you read it—and get into action—your life will obviously never be the same again for the better.

The Obvious will give you the tools that allow you to design a life you deserve!

This is Les Brown, Mrs. Mamie Brown's baby boy
Motivational Speaker / Author / Coach / Entrepreneur

Contents

Introduction 1

PART I

Do the Obvious to Live the Dream 5

1. What is the Obvious? _____ 7
2. The Obvious is Universal _____ 9

PART II

The Obvious Universal Laws for Business Success 61

3. The Obvious Law of Focus _____ 65
4. The Obvious Law of Planning _____ 71
5. The Obvious Law of Resource Management _____ 77
6. The Obvious Law of Innovation & Change _____ 83
7. The Obvious Law of Communication _____ 89
8. The Obvious Law of Accountability _____ 95
9. The Obvious Law of Productivity & Work Quality _____ 101
10. The Obvious Law of Personal Character & Belief _____ 107
11. The Obvious Law of Team Power _____ 113
12. The Obvious Law of Negotiating _____ 119
13. The Obvious Law of Mentorship & Practice _____ 125
14. The Obvious Law of Service _____ 131

PART III

The Obvious Universal Laws in Action 137

15. Live the Dream _____ 139
16. Powerteam International _____ 145
17. Take Action Now _____ 147

Introduction

If you're like most people, you want success...and you want success *yesterday*. Success in business and in life takes work. Sometimes people want to bypass the work and look for "the secrets" to just have the success with minimal effort. It doesn't work that way. There are things you need to do to get results. By learning from others who have achieved at the level you desire, you can achieve success more rapidly. The Obvious is about the work and dedication it takes to live your dreams.

My name is Bill Walsh. My vision is to empower others to live their dreams. Part of that vision is to provide mentoring opportunities for people like you who are ready for massive success! That's why I established Powerteam International. Powerteam provides venture capital funding, high level business coaching, integrated learning programs, inspirational workshops and personal development training for entrepreneurs and business owners. As the President & CEO, I am driven to make a difference for others every day.

I know what it's like to be massively successful...and what it's like to be broke. I grew up on the south side of Chicago. My family was great, but we certainly didn't have material success. Both of my parents worked 40 hours a week to make money and provide for 5 kids. My life began to change when I was in my teens and was fortunate enough to spend time with families that lived on the other side of money! They could afford to spend weekends doing what they wanted, where they wanted and with whom they wanted. What a concept! I began to learn then that it takes think-ing differently and taking different actions to achieve success. I achieved much success at such an early age, that when I bought my first home and car the neighbors thought my parents bought it for me! I also know what it looks like to be broke. It is not FUN! When the tough times come along you will find that your true friends walk in when everyone else walks out!

Even after achieving success, there are ongoing challenges to overcome. Because I have overcome (and continue to overcome) many challenges and look for opportunities to help others achieve even more success, I know what it takes firsthand to live the Obvious. That's part of what gives me the credentials and the drive to show other people what it takes.

One of the ways to make a difference was to write this book and reveal The Obvious—in plain sight—to show you what it takes to achieve success. This book provides a comprehensive look at *specifically* what it takes to breakthrough your biggest challenges and how to live your biggest dreams!

This book will give you the keys to make success happen by identifying the Obvious Universal Laws for Business Success. Once you know what they are, you can put them into action to get the results you want.

This book is organized into three parts: *Part I - Do The Obvious to Live The Dream* tells about the Obvious; *Part II – The Obvious Universal Laws for Business Success* tells about the individual *Obvious* Laws that work together for successful results; and *Part III – The Obvious Universal Laws in Action* tells how to get them in action to live the dream by taking action now. Some parts may have repetition because I really want you to get that part.

At Powerteam International, we are dedicated to giving you the tools to do the Obvious (and even the not-so-*Obvious* ones) to expedite your success.

Let's get started!

I hope you enjoy the journey!

Bill Walsh

PART I

Do the Obvious
to Live the Dream

1
What is the Obvious?

This book is called *The Obvious: Universal Laws for Business Success* because there are *Obvious* practices that are so universal that they have become like laws you must do to be successful in business. Without them, you will not achieve success. People often look for secrets to success rather than recognize The Obvious and do them.

So, what is "The Obvious"? The Obvious can be summed up like this: it is virtually hidden from people's view because people don't like the answer. The answer is that they actually do have to do the work. One of the core secrets is that you actually have to build great relationships and invest in your future everyday. That's where most people miss the mark. Relationships are a foundational part of service, which is key for all business success but the long term success is based on the follow up and follow through!

That's where it comes back to the Obvious. You've got to see the things that are *Obvious*. Most people do see them. They're just not present to them. When you become more present to the Obvious and The Universal Laws for Business Success introduced in this book, it's amazing how much more success you have. It's remarkable how many more doors open up, and how much better you feel about where you are...and where you're going.

Recognizing the obvious work required is another key to success as you begin to go through the entire process. It's a foundational key, though, so you will not fight the process because there will be ups and downs. You'll begin to see that clues are certainly easy to find when you're focused on the big picture, but you've got to break it down to master the mundane. Then, you have to make sure your team sees the same vision. Vision drives it through.

This book gets you on the right track so that you can open yourself up to learning more of the right things to do. Do the Obvious and begin living your DREAMS!

2
The Obvious is Universal

Now that you know that the Obvious is work, it is easy to see that the Obvious is also universal. Lots of people work in businesses or organizations of their own or those that others own. The type of work that gets done and how it gets done produces the results. If you don't like the results you're getting, change what you're doing. It's that simple. Many people want success, but overlook what it really takes to make it happen. This book will point you in the right direction.

This chapter in particular describes how to: Be Inspired by Your Vision; Find Power in Your Why; Believe in Yourself; Get Yourself Accountable; Dance with Challenges; Be Consistently Persistent; and Pay It Forward. These are all key to the Obvious laws of Success, which are universal.

There are various ways to do the "how-to's" for doing the Obvious work. Some ways are more efficient than others. Even though many people know about the Obvious, they still do not do what it takes to achieve success.

Decide now. Do the Obvious, Live the Dream! It all starts with your vision.

Be Inspired by Your Vision

Do you require motivation to succeed daily? Which do you think is better: Motivation or Inspiration? You know it's a great question because I hear a lot about how you have to motivate your sales-people. You do need to motivate people to have success, but motivation by itself is not the answer.

My challenge with motivation being key comes down to this scenario: if you take a group of people that are idiots and you motivate them, what do you have? That's right. You've got a group of motivated idiots.

See, I don't believe that motivation by itself is the answer. I think so often that if you're motivating people that's one thing, but what happens if you motivate someone that is going downhill? What have you just done? You only speed them up in the direction they're headed and they crash even faster! I see it in business where people go to an event, read a book, or listen to an audio series—and they get all motivated. Motivation by itself really is an empty fix for the real issue. The real issue for people is that they don't need motivation. What they need is education. They need hope, education and inspiration.

You see, motivation might get people temporarily excited. Maybe having a sales rep at your auto dealership or some type of business where they've got to sell something *right now* will benefit from being motivated daily.

For most people, though, it's actually inspiration that's most essential.

Inspiration truly starts with the power of your language. You see, many people do understand that what truly provides the foundation for success is the quality of your communication.

So, if you want to have even more success, like having better relationships or making more money, look at the quality of your ability to effectively communicate. Where does that start? It starts with education. It starts with hope, education and inspiration.

When many successful people are asked the question, "What motivates you?" They answer, "I don't need motivation."

In an interview with Tony Robbins, he was asked, "Tony, what motivates you when it comes to doing all the things you do?" You know what he said? He said, "My vision is so strong it actually pulls me towards my goals." His vision inspires him into action.

That's what I'd like you to focus on. Take a moment and stop focusing on being motivated; and start focusing on getting inspired about what you're doing. Write down what inspires you to get into action.

What is your VISION?

_____

_____

_____

_____

Sometimes what you find inspiring can change—but when you truly find a vision that is deeply inspiring for you, it inspires you over and over again in a way that drives you into taking action.

Where does inspiration come from? Inspiration comes from tapping into your spirit that's inside. Enthusiasm comes from your spirit. It comes from having the passion that actually pulls you to create more success versus just being excited. I don't believe that people who are merely excited are going to have long-term success. They may be motivated and have success that day.

Short-term motivation is the big problem I see with the diet companies. Why do most of these diets fail for most people, yet keep them trying the same types of diets over and over? The answer is because they get motivated to lose that weight and to look like the person on the TV screen, so they look for a quick fix to lose the weight quickly—while they're still motivated. The motivation wears off. Rather than motivation and quick fixes that don't last, people who want to lose weight need to get inspired about physical fitness and being in great shape! Being inspired changes the language they use and their actions to get a good education about weight-related topics like nutrition and exercise. Inspiration from the inside will help get you on a solid path to success! VISION is the driver that elevates your inspiration everyday to achieve the most outrageous goals ever imaginable. Have faith IT WORKS!

Here's another example about motivation. All the time, I see people get motivated to make money. I ask people, "What motivates you?" They say things like, "Making $2,000, $5,000, $20,000 a month. I'd be really motivated."

That may motivate them in the short-term. For most people, it is a false sense of accomplishment because, they hit the goal that month, but then the next month they go right back down. The reason is, once again, they are not truly inspired. They are not coming from a place where they're inspired to understand the power of their communication and of their language and the true driver that will move them to consistent daily, weekly and monthly success!

You see, it's better to make a statement than to ask the motivation question. Start your statement with these two words: I AM. That's right, I am. In your thoughts, use statements like: I am even more successful. I am going to do an even better job of getting to the health club. I am going to do an even better job of eating healthy. That's where it truly starts. If you want to have a lot of success at whatever it is that you're doing, look at the quality of your language.

Is your language inspiring you to move towards that outcome? Or are you just motivated? If you're just motivated, it's not going to work. It's not going to last. You'll have to have more motivation. That's why you've got to keep going back and buying more of that product, or this, or attend more seminars because you're just motivated. Stop buying shelf help and go to the SOURCE of your success – tap into your VISION today and begin seeing life for what it truly is – magical, divine and omni-possible!

The true inside, the true success, starts with being inspired. You have to have an inspiring vision with a strong enough reason as to why you are driven to achieve. Inspiration will last and so will the actions and the results when it is directed towards a powerful vision that you are in alignment with! (Write that down and read it daily.)

Now, how do you tap into that portal of inspiration? Once again, you've got to start by taking a stand on the inside so that your passion begins to shine through on the outside! This is where the success begins, and tapping into your vision is what begins and fuels the long term process of winning! When your vision becomes so strong that you don't want to sleep, eat, watch TV or anything that is not related to your highest purpose then you know you are on track! Focus on giving yourself better language and better communication to go out there and achieve those dreams – that's where it starts. That's just the beginning.

As you begin to live inspired, you will begin to look at the way you communicate and use language regarding money, love and success! We all know money is only one thing— money is only energy. That's all it is. In it's simplest form money comes down to, energy. Your language about money creates the energy that surrounds the value you create in the marketplace today!

If you want to make more money, create more value.

If you want to have better things in your life, create more value. What does it mean to "create more value"? It means, start with the process of having a great value proposition with the service and/or product that you provide. Then, become even more inspired about what you offer! Finally go out there and achieve your biggest dreams! Tell yourself everyday IT'S POSSIBLE! Success starts with your commitment and it often means you have to get up early and go to bed late.

SUCCESS IS A PROCESS NOT AN EVENT!

It's really about getting educated and owning the recipe of success.

Inspiration gets you started and will keep you going especially when times are tough and remember tough times will come!

Always remember...Tough times don't last but tough people do!

When you're inspired from a great vision, you will design an unstoppable blueprint to actually go out there and do the things you've dreamed about doing! When you drive from a great vision, the inspiration will move you along and actually <u>pull</u> you to have even more success in every area of your life!

Take the story of Steve Wynn. Here's a great example! He started as a bellhop in the 60's in Las Vegas parking cars. He moved up to dealing blackjack and then owning part of a casino. Next, he INVESTED his time and money into that hotel group and later sat on the Board of Directors. He went on to building some of the nicest casinos in all of Las Vegas such as The Mirage, and Treasure Island. After that he built the 2 billion dollar hotel, "The Bellagio", which is one of the finest casinos in the world. But here's a crazy stat that most people don't know, he's legally blind. What does he have that most people with 20/20 eyesight will never have? You are right. He has great vision. That's what you have to have to WIN and succeed in business in today's marketplace!

IT IS TAPPING INTO YOUR VISION WITH PASSION AND PURPOSE THAT WILL SET YOU FREE! STOP COMPLAINING ABOUT YOUR NEEDS AND FOCUS ON WHAT YOU HAVE! YOU HAVE GREATNESS IN YOU!

NOW IS THE TIME TO LET THAT GREATNESS SHINE BRIGHTLY!

You really have to set aside the motivation part, and instead have the understanding that when you when you come from a place of inspiration and empowering language, it'll move you to achieving those goals and those dreams that are most important in your life.

You should be living your dreams everyday! Your time on this planet is so brief – it is a shame not to make it count!

Stop counting the days and make the days count!

Do you know the location of some of the greatest ideas in the world, some of the greatest books, and some of the greatest businesses? They're in the cemetery because people never took the time to go out there and really embark on their dreams to live their vision and realize their full potential.

But that's *not you. YOU ARE AMAZING!*

When you understand the power of the Obvious, the Obvious says to take a really good look inside and use empowering language to win on the outside. Then, you tap into your vision and go out there and achieve it. Because your vision is so strong, it will actually pull you toward your goals. You don't need motivation because you are so excited about your life and because you're coming from a place of service to help others and you're making a difference. So, when it comes down to what's more important –motivation or inspiration – I vote for inspiration.

HOW DO YOU TAP INTO YOUR VISION? – Your values have to be in alignment with your actions to be on path and purpose to succeed! Take a moment and walk through this exercise! Always remember when you ask better questions you will get better answers!

VALUES

TODAY--------------------------12/24 Months from Today

ACTIONS

Find the Power in Your Why

"If your why is strong enough, you'll figure out the how!"

—Bill Walsh

What a concept! But, what does it really mean, "If your why is strong enough, you'll figure out the how?"

The strength of your PERSONAL WHY that you have on the inside will be the difference maker on your ability to break through the big challenges you will definitely face on the outside. There are challenges along the way to becoming successful and wealthy. The challenges you're going to face will define your character and mold the person you become on the outside! The strength of your why inside of you is what will truly get you through the toughest times you will face in life!

For me, without a doubt, My Why is about my kids—Austin, Marissa and Evan. My Why is also about creating things at a higher level. It's about inspiring the planet and inspiring business owners to make better decisions from a place of love instead of fear. It's about giving back to our military. It's about making a significant difference of leaving a legacy that really empowers people even though I'm gone.

When I look at successful businesses and companies, that success definitely starts with companies determining their why and then figuring out the how.

WHAT IS YOUR PERSONAL WHY?

_____

_____

_____

As you start to look at the challenges you are going to face, I always recommend that you take a few moments to write down your answer to these two simple questions:

1) What business are you in?

2) Why are you doing it?

The second question asking "Why" is truly more important than the "What" because if the why is not strong enough, when you face those inevitable challenges, and hit those road bumps, you'll quit. You're going to go out into the marketplace thinking you've got all the answers and all of a sudden—"Bam!"— you're going to hit some walls. Be ready for the challenges that life will bring and be ready to dance in the face of adversity!

If you looked at business success like a 100-yard football field, what happens is that by the first 20-yard line, most entrepreneurs quit and close their new business. Part of the Obvious is recognizing that you will have those challenges, but learning and applying the Laws of the Obvious described in this book will give you the big picture as well as the mundane steps on how to overcome them.

When you get out there and have those challenges, the power of Your Why will drive you to overcome them. The power of Your Why starts with your spirit, it starts on the inside. If you truly have an inspiring why that moves you, your spirit will move you to take action to help you get to where you're going. I don't believe it is motivation. I believe it's the why that becomes part of your bigger vision. As your vision and your why become really strong, it actually pulls you. Now you know where to find the power that will help you overcome any obstacle in life or business that you face!

If you have kids, think about this for a second. Would you run into a burning building to save your kids? Would you do whatever it takes? There's no doubt in my mind you would. Anyone would.

TAP INTO THE POWER OF YOUR INNER-SPIRIT TO WIN!

But in your business, are you doing whatever it takes? Are you getting up early? Are you going to bed late? Are you thinking about who you are, where you are and where you're going, and with whom?

When you know you're coming from that place of service, success is right around the corner. When you know you're building some-thing special that serves many then you will instantly realize that the success you are looking for is right around the corner. That's a problem with many people who start off striving for success. They lose the passion. They lose the spark for success!

Well, I can tell you what re-ignites the spark and re-ignites the passion is having a really big why. You know, Mother Teresa talked about how she would never go to an anti-war rally, but she was the first one to show up at a peace rally. Her Why was about peace and love. Her actions demonstrated that, including where she chose to spend her time and who she chose to be around or not.

So in your life, please rewrite your big why?

Take a moment to write it out here. Just begin to write from your heart.

- Ask yourself:

  o "What truly inspires me about my life today?"

  o "What gets me excited about what I'm doing now and what I want to be doing?" Is it the people in my life? Is it family? Is it a cause?

My Why behind My Vision

Date: _____

My Vision is...

_____

_____

My Why that drives me to pursue My Vision is...

_____

_____

_____

_____

Your answers will have to come from the inside. There are so many possibilities and opportunities you could pursue. Being able to be focused starts by you searching within yourself to determine what's most important so that when distractions come along that you will own the path your on and will dismiss all distractions!

That's why it is so important that you anchor this concept of Your Why. You've got to have that empowering Why which will drive you to pursue your dream with passion and purpose! Your Why will empower you to overcome big challenges so you can win the big opportunities.

Always REMEMBER

The bigger the challenge the bigger the opportunity!

In business, it's reasons and results. What I believe creates the results for those who are champions is that they start with an empowering Why that's non-negotiable. They have a posture based on absolute belief and faith in the place that where they are. It drives them from the inside to have all the success on the outside.

So, if you want to have more fun, if you want to make more money, if you want to make a difference on this planet, take a moment and really empower Your Why.

One of the programs offered through Powerteam International is called *The Rainmaker Summit* where you are taught how to tap into and empower Your Why. Not just any Why, though. It's Your Why that truly drives what it is you want to achieve...and, of course, why you want to achieve it. You will build a movie about your why with pictures, images, words and music that express it...and inspires you.

I cannot emphasize this point enough. It's really important because it is the fuel that will drive you to continue, even during the toughest, challenging times because as a business owner, as a parent, as an entrepreneur, and as a business partner, you're going to have the big challenges. I certainly have. That is why I can speak from experience about what it takes and how to truly win.

My invitation to you is to take the time to become so inspired about who you are as a person, where you are now, and where you're going.

The secret to the Obvious is understanding how to put all these principles and practices into motion *from Day One*.

I can also tell you that success is *a process* – not an event. Power-team International (www.pti360.com) is committed to providing the necessary tools and programs to help entrepreneurs and business owners worldwide with what it takes to be successful (PTI events are where you can learn, network, connect and grow to continue that process of increasing your successfulness).

You are well on your way to creating more success and having more fun along the way. It's important to enjoy the journey and to help others as you go because as you do, you make the world a better place by inspiring one person at a time to really go out there and make a difference. Once again, the Obvious is the true secret of creating wealth in your life. It definitely starts with discovering and staying inspired by being sure Your Why is empowering and in alignment with who you are on the inside! If you don't like the results you are having in your life right now today – it is the perfect time to look inside to make the changes you plan to see on the outside!

Believe in Yourself

If you don't believe in yourself, how do you expect others to believe in you?

You have to begin with the non-negotiable posture. You've got to start with the belief in the saying that "I am. I am successful. I AM EVEN MORE SUCCESSFUL" Unleash your greatest you today!

Don't talk about want...or try...or maybe...or I'm going to get to it later. Winners and champion, start with these two simple words: "I am." If your belief system is non-negotiable, if your focus and your passion is non-negotiable, people will know that.

Did you ever notice that when positive people come in the room that the light brightens up and the room becomes brighter? Yet, when negative people come in the room, the lights go dim and the room dampens. They're so negative. Do you know some of those negative people?

Let me tell you something, they're dream killers. The good news is, there are only about six of those negative people in the whole world. They just get around a lot.

If you're thinking about what it takes to live those dreams and to have that success, you've got to have a belief system that starts on the inside. You see, you'll never have success on the outside until you have success on the inside.

23

So, think about your own belief system today. Do you have those negative anchors? Are you running on old programs? That's what most people do because they're programmed at a very, very young age to be told things like: "You're dumb;" "You're stupid;" or "You're an idiot."

You've got to break through all that stuff. The key to breaking through it is to turn off the negative TV. That's right! If you want to raise your income, make more money, and live a better lifestyle, turn off the negative TV programming because all it does is desensitize you. It is designed to keep you entertained, stupid and powerless! Today is your day to start living your dreams!

Think about it. If you wake up to negative, go to bed to negative— what do you think you become? No, not just negative...you become *really* negative. And what are negative people like? Think about it this way: have you ever heard the saying that misery loves, what? Misery loves company, right? No. It is not misery loves company. It is misery loves *your* company.

You see, if your belief system is so strong, those negative people will tend to get out of the way. Think about it. If you have ever met amazing people, you notice how they just shine as they come through the space. It is because their inner belief system will not allow the negative surroundings to slow them down. A lot of times in life it is not what happens to you, it is how you react to what happens to you. But that starts with how strong are you are on the inside.

How resilient are you to all the negative factors that you encounter every day? If you are ready for that, you are going to break through because you have got to be tougher than the adversity you face. If not, the adversity is going to win.

When you study successful people and when you study people that have not had that success—the only difference is that when they fell down, the winners got back up because their belief system told them to get back up and keep going for success.

When you start with yourself, start with your inner being and start with the voices that come through you. When your subconscious mind is in program (and I really do mean "program," where your values and your actions are congruent), imagine how your path and your purpose are absolutely unstoppable. When they are in sync, then you are in sync. When you are in sync, people around you will notice that.

So, you have had a challenge with getting on path and getting on purpose. When that happens, look at one thing...your highest values. Chunk it up to the highest level. What is totally most important in your life?

Next, look at your actions. Are your actions congruent with those values you hold? If they are not, you are going to be out of integrity. The only way you are going to break through and achieve all the dreams you are looking for is that you have got to be congruent from the inside. You have got to start with that inner spirit. That is where enthusiasm comes from. Did you know that?

Your belief system is the core that drives it all. It starts with the reprogramming in your mind. You've got to start in your mind; and you've got to start in your heart. They have to be in total alignment to achieve massive success!

Then, what all of a sudden starts to happen is your beliefs go to work on the world and the universe, which will literally yield to your belief system if you understand the power of what's possible. It's scary that it takes miracles to happen—like a jet landing in the Hudson River—for us to say it's a miracle.

Listen, miracles happen every day. But are you present for them? When you tap into your belief system, when you own the space that you come from, when you absolutely understand that your values are congruent with the highest level of your actions, you'll tap into that inner strength, that inner being that will light up and take you to the next level.

That is the key to understanding how I live that unbelievable lifestyle and really having the things that most people talk about but people never get the chance to really live. That's the secret: tap into your belief system. Believe in yourself when nobody else does. Then, get totally focused on where you are going and who is going there with you. You don't have to be rich to be wealthy! I am blessed to have great friends and my health – that is wealthy!

Build a Good Team

Well, the Obvious answer to living your dream is to build a good team. I know that sounds really simple. You've probably heard all the clichés, like:

"There's no 'I' in team."

"You can't do it by yourself. You have to build a really great team."

"I hire really smart people."

Whether you love Donald Trump or you hate him, it doesn't matter. You know what he's really good at doing? He's great at assembling phenomenal teams. Take a moment and look at your business or look at things you're attempting to create. Instead of doing it alone, start to think about who would be included on the best team that you could put together.

I had a chance to spend some time with Eric Davis from The San Francisco 49ers. It was really neat because he told me a story about how every year when the season started he and the team would walk through the stadium. As they walked, the only thing they focused on was winning a championship. It needs to be the same thing in your company.

Are you the best in class who does everything that it takes to really be # 1 in your space? When you launch a company or launch a business, you want people to think of you when they think of integrity, class, style, service and great experience. Well, it starts with building a great team.

A question I often get asked is, "How do I bring a great team together?" New companies especially have this concern. Because they are a new company, they often don't have the money and ask how they can afford a great team.

How do we find phenomenal people to be a part of our vision, our dream, and our plan? Well, there are many companies out there you can study. One is a company called EMC; and another company is like Enterprise Rent-A-Car. What it comes down to is to hire people who really understand your vision first so they can be coming from a place of service where if they're bringing lots of value to the company, you pay them lots of money.

I know this isn't easy for a lot of companies. You're probably thinking, "We can't afford a team. We're just not sure." Let me tell you something, you can't afford <u>not</u> to go out there and pay the most money you can for great help. And the reverse is true that you can never pay too little for the bad help you may have received in the first place. So often this happens, right? People always pay too little for bad help. That's a big mistake.

You want to focus on going to the marketplace right? Bring in a great vision and a great brand that inspires people to be a part of your cause. I did some homework and I checked on a company called Zappo's and a gentleman named Tony Hsieh. He focused on creating an incredible culture for their business. You should research the work they did and how see how he built a billion dollar business in just 8 years!

You are only as good as the team you build! It is a wonderful story!

Please take a moment and write down specifically how you're building your business. You should start with the concept of what it takes to build a Superbowl franchise team! Write down exactly who you're looking for and how they will help you take your business, your brand, and your message global. Don't forget, you're in a global economy today. You're competing for global dollars. Your customers vote with their dollars!

You've got to do a phenomenal job of creating that value. It all starts with how good your team is. When Tony Hsieh and his team would hire people at Zappo's, they would ask questions related to two different areas: (1) Is this person qualified for the skill set required? Does this person have the aptitude? Can they really do the job at a high level? (2) Is this person service-oriented? Could this person be a hostess or a waiter?

Once again, focus on the power of your vision. Tap into your potential partners mindsets by sharing with them your vision! When you connect with the right people at a higher level they will get your message instantly. The SECRET to reach people at the highest level, is not about the money but the the combination of instant income and long term potential with your company! You have to create the value – short and long term!

Yes, you've got to pay them great money, but if they produce, you want to pay them <u>really</u> great money. Again, it's not just the money. What's also so important for so many people is the recognition combined with great compensation.

You see, recognition is a key thing for a lot of people. Go back in history, right? People would work for money, but they would die for a cause. So, think about that, for just one minute. Do you have a recognition program for your top producers? Think about your company today. What is the cause that you stand behind? As you know in business, people are looking for something to stand for and believe in. I found that if you build something with a solid foundation, your team has the best chance to win.

You could be in restaurants, you could be in network marketing, or you can name any company you want to, but you've got to really take a moment and say, "You know what? If I could build a Superbowl franchise team as I'm building my company, who's going to be a part of that team? Who am I going to let in?" I'll give you the specifics that'll help you bring them to your company:

- Provide a big vision that inspires people.

- Establish a platform where they can really be rewarded for providing value.

- Create a great culture of winners who want to work together, play together, and have lots of fun while building something great.

When it is all said and done, making a lasting difference for the world is what matters most. PLEASE never forget you have to make a profit to stay in business!

Get Yourself (and Your Team) Accountable

The only way to truly win in business can be summed up in one word. That one word is: Accountability. I know as an entrepreneur, as a business owner, many dislike this word. Business owners do not like the word "accountability" – but it is obviously the key element relating to every aspect of business. Accountability starts with you!

Now, could you ever imagine opening a McDonald's franchise by investing a couple of million dollars, yet having no cash registers? Or could you ever imagine having a company where the store was open all day, yet you never track the sales?

What I have found by studying companies is that the reason accountability is so important is that it helps you schedule your success. If you are not accountable, you do not schedule or plan what it takes to succeed.

As a result, by default, you plan your failure.

Look at the numbers out there today. More than 90 percent of companies in the United States fail in the first 2 years. Why is that? They never take the time to actually set the foundation. It serves as the blueprint for them to actually follow through. Instead, they guess about the amount of money they will need, the marketing strategy and so many other key elements necessary to succeed in today's marketplace. It is very sad!

As I have traveled around the world and actually worked with a variety of companies and businesses, one of the common ingredients that I have found in the recipes for success is that those that have a lot of success track it. So if you want to have more success in your business, there are several basic things you must put in place. One of those keys is you have to have a great plan to track the success.

There are different elements that need tracking because they provide feedback for you to know how you are doing. Tracking could start with something very simple like Daily Sales. Every day you could ask yourself, "How much did I sell today?" And then begin to scorecard it day after day... after day...after day.

Eventually, your daily tracking will provide you with enough data that you will begin to observe the trends. In business (and really anything you are doing), you have got to be willing to be open to studying the trends.

So, as you are getting your company started, you should look at the numbers. And, of course, you could always look at a checking account. That's always a good way, right? But I want to go a little deeper than that. I want you to understand that the power of accountability starts with you.

One of the processes that we teach is called "10 before 10." You may be asking yourself, "What does that mean, Bill? What is '10 before 10'?" Let me back up first before I answer that.

It's like I said earlier about how watching the TV every day makes you negative. <u>You</u> then become negative. You know how "misery loves company." No, actually, misery loves *your* company. You see, if you are successful and you are building things, they—the people you spend time with who become your usual company—do not want you to be successful.

But I'll tell you what drives it through the mediocrity to achieve success is <u>you</u> planning your success every day. So, "10 before 10" says this: Turn off the TV and watch your income go up. Every night, before you go to bed, what I would like you to do is write down your "10 before 10" for the next morning. These are the 10 Most Important Things that you will accomplish before 10:00 am the next morning. Yeah, this is "10 before 10."

And, I know this is not easy, but what starts to happen is you will get everything out of the way. You will get focused on what is truly most important to help you to create that success.

Just try "10 before 10." Try it for 14 days. It takes 14 days to create a habit. So, for 14 days, write out the 10 most important things. Study it. Get them done in the morning. No distractions. No distractions until those 10 things are done before 10:00 a.m. ...and watch what starts to happen. Everyday, make a list of your 10 most important things for that day. It could look as simple as this format:

My 10 Before 10 List

Today's Date: _____

#1 _____

#2 _____

#3 _____

#4 _____

#5 _____

#6 _____

#7 _____

#8 _____

#9 _____

#10 _____

Then, one by one, do the things on your list. Starting with the most important one, and continue until you have completed all of them. When you're done, reward yourself by doing something you enjoy for a moment.

You will have more quality time; you will have more fun; and you will be able to do the things you always talked about doing. So often I find as I look at companies that all important business owners are always busy—but nothing is getting done.

Instead of being busy, how about being productive? Are you ready to get more productive? By doing the most important things, you'll be more productive instead of just being busy with things that don't matter. It starts with you.

You see, your habits become your character. Your character becomes your destiny. And, once again, I know as an entrepreneur this is not easy, but accountability is the secret.

I will give you some ideas. I will give you a thought process for a second. If I were to give you $86,400 today, would you take it? The catch is that you have to spend it or invest it by the end of the day. Would you take it and could you do it? Of course you could!

What if I gave it to you again tomorrow? $86,400 dollars again. Again, though, you have got to spend it or invest it by the end of the day. Could you do it again?

How about another day? $86,400 again. Could you keep spending or investing that amount wisely day after day?

How about if you never knew when it was going to end. Could you continue to spend or invest it wisely?

Now, here's a better question: "What do you find is more valuable—time or money?"

Which is it for you? Time or Money?

Now, if you are young and you are reading this and getting some of the information, you might say, "Just give me the money. I've got plenty of time." But, in reality, most people would say that time is so much more valuable than money.

Now, think about this one for a minute: Every day you get 86,400 seconds. My question to you is: "Who do you spend the time with?"

What I would challenge you to do is to strengthen your accountability by getting a great Mastermind Team. Get rid of all of the negative people in your life. Get truly focused on creating more things by being around the right people. It has been said so many times, "Your net worth is equal to your network." Well, it all starts by having a great Mastermind Team.

I invite you to have two teams. That's right, two teams: one team that you help; and another team that helps you. You see, I learned this a long time ago:

"There is plenty of room at the top. It is the bottom that's overcrowded!"

So, what are you going to do differently today? What is going to look different so you are going to have more success tomorrow than you had today? More success next year than you had last year? You see, you have to do things differently. If you keep doing the same thing over and over and expect a different result it's a definition of what? You're right. Einstein said it best: "It's insanity."

Einstein also said that the only way you can raise the game – raise *your* game – is to go to a higher place for the answers.

When it comes to accountability, it comes down to YOU.

It comes down to the fact that you're the one that has to lead the national expansion for your company – but, it starts with you taking ownership of your Daily Method of Operation. That's right, your DMO.

What is your Daily Method of Operation? It is what you do and how you do it. Some of the big things, once again, include getting the "10 before 10" done; spend time with only quality people; and then begin to track your success.

NEVER GIVE UP ON YOUR DREAMS!

Here's an easy way for a new business to track success from *Day One*. Look at asking and answering these questions every day:

- How many new people do we prospect?

- How many new customers came in the business?

- How many new referrals did we get?

Because when you look at a company, the basic operation is two things:

- Acquire the customers.

- Retain the customers.

If you can do that well, you're going to build an amazingly successful company, have a lot of fun, and provide a lot of value to the market place. So, when it comes down to the bottom line, the bottom line is that "Everyone on your team—including you—has to be accountable to win in today's economy."

Expect Challenges

The greatest time for economic growth is when there are problems. When you can solve big problems, you can literally write your own ticket. You can write your check for the amount you want to be paid. But I can tell you that before you get there, if you're running a business, if you're growing a business, if you're thinking about launching a company, you are going to have those big challenges.

It's the same in life. You're going to have big challenges. You know the story about Donald Trump, right? He had lots of money. Well, true, he started with lots of money. But what he was noted for was one of the greatest turnarounds of all time. Around 1991, he literally was more than 900 million dollars in the hole. Big challenge, right?

Could he have just folded up and stopped? No. He said, "You know what? I'll put my head down; and I'll get focused; and I'll go to work." He realized how big the opportunity would then be when the economy turned again. And he was right!

You see, the thing to understand and remember is that the bigger the challenge, the bigger the opportunity. You have got to focus on change to change your environment.

As you're going through your business, and going through your life, and you're having ups and downs, here's the bottom line: you're not alone.

Everybody goes through that. I've had all kinds of great successes and great failures, but everybody does that. You're doing that at whatever stage you are in in your life. Never look at yourself as if you're unemployed. Instead, think about the fact that you're "in transition."

If your company is going through a downtime, don't think about: "If I just had money, I could solve the problem." Instead, I want you to think about: "If I create more value, will I bring more customers to the business?"

When you look at the challenges even our economy has gone through, it is not an instant quick fix. Realize that the American economy drives the global economy.   But what drives that? Everybody thinks it is big business. I'm here to tell you today that the success starts with small business America.

So, when you start talking about big challenges you're facing— they could be personal, they could be health-related, or they could be business related—what I find is that most of the challenges people deal with all start with stress. A lot of times that stress starts with the people you surround yourself with all the time.

How do you all of a sudden change that circle? When life comes at you in its toughest moment, it's either going to stare you down and knock you over—or you're going to stare it down and plow through it. When those big challenges show up, what I want you to think about is: "How do you bring in the wisdom to break through the challenge?" Not the wisdom to go around the challenge, but to go right through the challenge.

When you have that sense of direction that comes from having values and congruent actions, being on purpose and on path is the only way you break through the big challenges. I just want you to understand that with those challenges come the big opportunities.

If you're launching your business, if you're growing your business, or if you're going through the change of your business, realize this: one of the easiest ways to solve that problem is take a step outside your business.

So often we're so busy being in the business, we can't see what the business is doing. It's almost like going to that 30,000-foot level to see the big picture. Take a trip up to the sky (or maybe even two or three trips) to take a really good look at your business. Some things may be obvious from that view that you didn't see at the ground-level view.

What I've found is that when you've got those big challenges, surround yourself with brilliant people. To get through big challenges, you can never pay too much for good help...and you can never pay too little for bad help. So, it comes back to paying attention to who you surround yourself with, right?

If you don't like where things are, it is a great time to change. You know the most beautiful thing about breaking through big challenges? It's so rewarding on the other side. But...that's just the stepping stone to the next challenge, to the next thing you're going to do.

At the end of the day, when you really sum it all up, have you made a significant impact on the world? Have you made the world a better place because you were here?

I know you might think that your challenges are so big; but, you know, we have programs for folks dealing with their challenges. One evening we had a whole circle of people talking about their biggest challenge and their biggest opportunity. There were some pretty big challenges...until we heard the last story. All of a sudden, the rest of the challenges weren't that important. We had people who experienced bad setbacks from motorcycle crashes to losing all their money in the stock market to having to start over for any number of reasons. Everything imaginable that could go wrong had gone wrong for some people. And obviously, they made it through the challenge.

But the last story was shared by a woman who shared how she went in to get some surgery done for her eyes...and came out blind. Wow! You talk about square in the heart or right between the eyes. All of a sudden, the biggest problems we had experienced or were experiencing still were not that big anymore.

The hardest part is being able to step outside of your business and step outside of your life to get a third-party look at it. Sometimes, the best way to do that is to surround yourself with great people. Don't surround yourself with the people that only look up to you, because they probably don't have the answers. You want to surround yourself with people you really look up to. This is where you can learn the answers and get the support you need. Surround yourself with leaders that will challenge you!

When the big challenges show up (and they're going to show up), you're going to have those curves and those ups and downs. There's no way around it when you're running a business. But, when they do show up, surround yourself with a team that you look up to and that you absolutely respect. You know they come from a place of integrity; and you know they come from a place to help you with your business. It's one of the greatest ways to break through a challenge.

Here's the funny part of that last story shared. The woman who had some of the biggest challenges as a result of becoming blind after eye surgery had the greatest optimism.

You see, the way you break through the big challenges is, you have vision. If you can tap into your vision, your vision becomes much stronger than sight by itself.

I mentioned Steve Wynn earlier. He is one of the most successful entrepreneurs in all of this country. He has built hotels and land developments, including the new Wynn Resort. He started out in Las Vegas as a nothing; a nobody. But what does he have that most people don't have? He has great vision. They say that he's legally blind, but what does he have that's even more important than his sight? He has big vision.

So, if you want to capture the biggest challenge that you're facing, tap into your biggest vision. When you're vision is so strong that it pulls you towards your goals, it's amazing how all of a sudden the windows of opportunity open up and you're more present to what's possible.

If you come to that place where the shutters are up and you can't see through them, there's no way to break through those challenges. But sometimes, step outside the box, and go to that 30,000-foot level. Search for help from people you respect that are playing at a higher level. They are willing to help!

Tap into your true potential. Your true potential comes from your vision. When you tap the vision and plan to win, your values and actions must be congruent. Let me tell you what, those challenges are no longer challenges. You break through. Not only do you break through, but you will break through in style.

If you're dealing with those big challenges today, get ready for your next big success story. Get prepared for all that's possible. To do that may take a minute or may take a day, or may take a week.

BE PRESENT TO THE UNLIMITED POWER OF THE UNIVERSE! IT WORKS!

It scares me today that people will spend more time planning their vacation than they will in planning their finances. They'll take more time to plan a dinner party with people at their home for a little get together than they will planning the next two years of their career.

And that's why when a challenge shows up, you've got to be ready for that challenge. You've got to have inner strength, and the gumption to break through those adversities because they are going to show up. But it's entirely up to you. It starts with you; and it ends with you. But surrounding yourself with the right people will make all the difference in the world!

When your belief system is in check and you're totally on path and on purpose, all of a sudden...the big challenges are not so big anymore. Tell your head to take special note of this simple concept: "Anything is possible." Everything is possible when you believe in who you are, and where you are today...and more importantly, where you're going.

My good friend Les Brown is an author, speaker and a speech coach who shares his inspiring story as he inspires others to overcome challenges and live their dreams. I asked him to share the biggest challenge he ever faced. As he answered my question, he said that he's thought about it carefully, because a lot of people ask him that question. Here's what Les said:

"Let me share something with you. It's easy for me to speak to people; to organizations; to go out to prisons to reduce our recidivism rate; or to inspire children to see themselves in the future. That's easy for me to do. It's easy for me to work with someone to help them develop their voice.

But let me share with you the most difficult thing I've ever done and the biggest challenge I've ever faced: to believe that I could do it. You see, given my background—being born in an abandoned building on the floor, being labeled educable mentally retarded, being adopted, being without college training and failing twice in school—it was challenging for me to believe that I could do what I'm doing right now. I get to change people's lives, to earn millions of dollars, and to have my own company. I believe as we look at the world today and look at the situations and circumstances people find themselves in, I think what I once heard is true: "You don't get in life what you want. You get in life what you are." According to your faith, be it unto you.

Well, the automatic question right now is, "How did you break through the challenging circumstances?" Well, there are a variety of ways. But one of the ways is reading. You've got to study. You've got to change your thinking. You've got to change your software. The other is having goals beyond your comfort zone because in order to do something you've never done, you've got to become someone you've never been. Something else that is very important is the relationships you have. Whoever you hang around with, that's who you're going to become.

My mother used to say, 'Leslie...'

I said, 'Yes, Ma'am, Momma?'

She continued, 'Birds of a feather flock together. You run around with losers, you'll end up with losers.'

Who you spend time with affects your thoughts and your actions—and they affect your results. So, the main thing is to develop your mind. That's why reading and learning about the Obvious—and then doing it— is so important.

Be Consistently Persistent

Success takes persistence. Not just persistence that comes and goes, but persistence where you're consistently persistent. What does it mean to be consistently persistent? You know, it really comes down to what Les Brown says:

> "When you want something bad enough, you'll do the things today that other people just won't; and you'll have tomorrow what other people just won't have."

There's another saying by another smart and successful guy named Gary Player, who says,"What you'll find is that people who work the hardest tend to get the luckiest." He might have said it a little differently, but that's what he meant.

I think it's no different in life or in business. You know, if you really want to have success, if you really want to have the opportunities, or if you want to have what other people talk about as success, you've got to be willing to model yourself after what those people are doing. You see, most people, they're just not willing to pay the price. They want the success. They want the nice cars. They want the money. They want the lifestyle, but they don't want to do the work that it takes to get there.

Think about what it takes to be a professional athlete. People don't realize how small the number of people is who actually make a living in the world playing golf. I think it's less than 100 people, right? So, what does it take to have that success?

A young man walked up to Jack Nicklaus one day and said, "Jack, I want to golf just like you."

Jack said, "No, you don't."

He said, "Yeah, Jack. I want to be a professional. I want to play golf just like you. I want to be on the tour."

Jack said, "No, you really don't want to do that."

The young man said, "What do you mean I don't want to do that?"

Jack explained that the young man was not willing to pay the price in advance. You're not willing to hit 500 golf balls a day—sometimes in the morning, sometimes at night until your hands bleed. And that's what success is really about. They make it sound so easy. They make it seem like "Boom!" it just appears. It just doesn't work that way.

Yes, you've got to have the belief system. Yes, you've got to persevere through a lot of stuff. But, you've got to be consistently persistent. You've got to be someone that gets up early, stays up late, does the work, makes the phone calls, and is willing to literally go out there and do things that other people are not willing to do.

That takes us back to asking: "What is the Obvious?" It is the work it takes to achieve business success. People don't like the answer. It takes work to invest in the relationships that business success is built upon. There's a way to do the Obvious so that you're making a difference for others—and that difference drives you even more. It takes consistency.

When I talk about "consistently persistent," I don't mean to bug people. I don't mean to bother people. I mean to go out of your way to create value for them. And do it over and over and over and over.

Go out of your way to make your customer experience outstanding. Go out of your way to take the time to call your top 20% customers. Send them an email. Send them a letter. Send them a card. Do the things today that other people don't like to do. Show up for the conferences. Work on the inside. Always be working on the inside to have success on the outside. It's something that most people, once again, just don't like to do.

Here's another great example of what I'm talking about here. Have you ever joined a health club and never went? I know you've got the guilt card in your pocket. I mean, you talk about wanting to be in shape. You talk about wanting to go to the gym. But most people join the gym in January, and keep paying throughout the year for something they're not using. But they still want to be in great shape.

The secret to being in great shape—if that really is your goal—is to start with that intention. Start with the intention that, "I want to be in better shape." Here are two great stats for you: (1) 97% of people who hire a coach show up; and (2) 80% of people who belong to a team that works out show up. So, what is the Obvious secret to success here? Absolutely—you've got to show up. But you've got to do it consistently.

People say they want to be in great shape, yet they go to the gym one time. People say they want to be wealthy, so they go to a seminar one time. That's not what it's about. It's about consistently showing up. It's about consistently doing the work... and then going way beyond that.

You see, that's only the start of the equation. The next step is asking, "How do I create more value?" How do I go out of my way if my goal is to be in better shape or if my goal is to be in better health? Do I hire a nutritionist? You say, well I can't afford all of this stuff. I love what you're talking about, Bill. But I can't afford a coach. I can't afford a team.

You see, what I find is that successful people, figure out exactly how to do it. They ask different questions. And that's what you want to start doing. If you're not happy where things are at in your life, this would be a great time to ask some different questions. Get around some people that ask those questions that will challenge you.

So, you've got to look at your goals. Take a moment now to write down your top five goals. What are your top five goals for the next 30 days? They could be about health. It could be about money. They could be about any combination of interests. Whatever they are, they need to be about anything that is most important to you.

Top Five Goals

Goal #1:_____

Goal #2:_____

Goal #3:_____

Goal #4:_____

Goal #5:_____

Now, what you have to do is actually own the language that you've written it in. Map the language so you own it. So you know exactly where you are and exactly where you're going. And then, become unstoppable with at least doing the action.

You know, I watched an amazing video one time. It is a short video about a young man whose friends would laugh at him. It is such an important example about being focused, consistent, and persistent in following your dreams and what you're trying to accomplish or what you plan to accomplish.

This young man was part of a young high school football team. His friends would laugh at him and they'd laugh at the team because they didn't believe that they could have the success. The young man, who was a leader on the team, didn't believe anymore either. When the coach said saw that, he called on him. He said, "Come over here, young man. I'm going to have you do the bear crawl." (You know, where someone gets down and crawls on their hands and feet.) The coach told him, "I want you to crawl to the 50-yard line." His friends all laughed at him.

And that's what's going to happen to you, right? As you're getting your business started, some people are going to laugh at you. "Oh, you joined that home-based business company?" "Oh, you're launching your company?" "That is never going to work." "You're going to fail."

He said, "Young man, I want you to put a blindfold on. I want you to do this wearing a blindfold."

The young man asked, "A blindfold? You know I can't do this."

The coach said, "Listen, just follow my direction. Just follow my lead and listen to my voice." When the coach added that the young man had to do it carrying someone on his back, his friends laughed even louder.

Just like in this scenario, your friends are going to laugh at you louder until you have lots of success.

So, while carrying the other football player on his back and wearing the blindfold, the young man put his head down and started to do the bear crawl as he walked and walked one step at a time. All of a sudden, he reaches the 20-yard line and was ready to collapse. His friends were laughing and saying put downs like: "You're not going to make it. You better quit now."

Yet, he kept listening to the encouragement of his coach telling him to keep going. He got to the 30-yard line, the 40-yard line, and the 50- yard line. He started going down the other direction towards the other goal line. He was literally ready to quit and exhausted. He couldn't see where he was on the field. He just persevered one step at a time.

Now, all of a sudden, the people that laughed at him were standing up in support of him. And that's going to happen to you when you start to have success. The same people that knocked your success will become your biggest raving fans.

And sure enough, he got over the goal line because the coach pushed him and pushed him and pushed him. When he collapsed on the goal line, he totally collapsed with exhaustion. Then, he got up and said, "You know coach, I've got to be at the 20- yard line, or the 40-yard line, or the 50-yard line by now."

The coach said, "Look up, son. You're in the end zone." Then he told the young player that he needs him to believe in himself and believe in the team so that they can have the success.

You've made the success. But you have to understand that in your business it's you who has to motivate and push yourself, as if you are your own coach. It's the same thing as having the coach that pushes you. You're the leader of your team. You're the inspirational force in your team. You're the one that has to drive the success when nobody else wants to do it.

It means, if you've got to be the janitor, if you've got to be the clerk, if you've got to be the person who answers the phone, if you've got to be the person that does whatever it takes to have that success, then it's you that has to do it. It all starts with you. That's being consistently persistent.

Howard Hughes went through the same challenge. He had a lot of success. Before he bought a lot of companies, he went and worked on the front lines. You may not know it, but he actually was a baggage handler for TWA airlines because he wanted to see what the employees had to go through. He wanted to learn from the bottom up.

That's one of the greatest things I learn from people like that. What do the most successful people do consistently? They go way out of their way, right? They go way out of their way to understand the growth curves of their business and the challenges in their business. Your company is only as good as your weakest link.

That's where it comes back to the Obvious. You've got to see the things that are obvious. When you become more present to the

"How to Connect with Millionaires"? No, of course not–because they didn't offer it.

When opportunity shows up for most people, you know what they do? They freeze. If I dropped you into a room full of millionaires and billionaires and I said go connect with them, you would probably be full of fear of what to say and how to interact.

I'll teach you to understand this process of connecting with high level people with absolute faith. That's right, with absolute faith. There's no room for fear.

But what does that come down to? What does that really back up into? It means that if you truly want to understand the true power of giving, go out there and "Pay It Forward" and expect nothing in return.

If you want to elevate your business, how do you connect with those people? What would you say if you got dropped into a room with highly successful people? One of the core secrets is not doing what most people do when they meet successful people.

What they do (that you don't want to do) is to start babbling all about themselves. Here's my car; here's what I do; here's my business; and on and on. That doesn't work. What does work is to ask them about themselves and <u>listen for ways to create value first and expect nothing in return.</u> Then, follow up on providing that value.

Here's a great example. More than five years ago, I had a chance to meet a gentleman named Mark Victor Hansen. As one of the co-authors of *Chicken Soup for the Soul* ® series, he's written lots of successful books.

When I met him, I said hello and shook his hand at a charity fundraiser. I donated to their charity because I knew he is someone who lives in a place of brilliance. His focus is to help the world, inspire the planet, and make the world a better place—and do it every day. I loved what he was about and his message.

After we met, nothing really happened. I didn't have the right connections or the right way to open the door. A year went by. Then two years went by. All of a sudden, it finally happened. We made a meaningful connection during the middle of 2009. That's when Mark and I had a chance to connect through another gentleman by the name of Robert Allen. They were writing a new book and would most likely be coming to Chicago as part of their book tour. I let them know that I believed in them and their message.

I told them that if they were coming to Chicago, I'd love to help promote their book. I added that as a matter of fact, I could probably put a group together who I'm sure would buy whatever books they brought. I asked for nothing in return. They didn't call back right away. They weren't sure if they would be in Chicago. A month went by and soon it was two weeks before the event.

One of the things required to become successful is to be persistent. So, I called again to follow up. It was just a few days before they were going to be in Chicago. They said that they did need my help in putting together a lunch. I let them know that we would buy whatever books they brought.

So, I got focused and made calls to more than one hundred people I knew I could count on to be at the lunch, even though it was with a last-minute notice. I let everyone I invited know the details of the event and that they *absolutely* had to be there.

Because I had previously done a great job of creating value for my friends and my associates, I was able to pull together the event quickly so that Mark Victor Hansen and Robert Allen could spend time with some world-class people who are literally making a difference on the planet.

When Mark and Bob showed up, they were totally blown away with how the whole room was full on a short notice. This event was the first time Mark Victor Hansen and I were formally introduced. He was blown away by the quality of the people who were there. Literally every book that they brought—and they brought cases of all of their books—was sold.

They asked how I could have pulled together such an event in just three days. I explained that it's because I created massive value first. By making it a best practice to create massive value, it becomes a habit and it builds upon itself.

Once again, when you create a lot of value, people understand that. I never asked them for anything, but what it developed into was a relationship where now Mark participates in much of our events. We've done so many great projects together as a result of one of the core secrets of success, "Pay It Forward."

I know it may not be easy to stomach that process because we're programmed otherwise. But as you start to live it, you'll start to realize how simple it is. Then, you'll realize how big the universe is and how the universe truly yields what's possible because you believe it's possible. Create the value in the market place, and then all of a sudden the universe starts to yield.

Here's another example. It happened another time where we were down. We, the Chicago Bears, were going to The Superbowl. Talk about Pay It Forward first, help other people first, and expect nothing in return.

A group of us went to The Ritz Carlton in Florida right before the Bears were going to play. We were sitting down talking and drinking a green new energy drink we were working with that helps relieve stress. We were feeling stress about how the Bears would play.

One of the green drinks was sitting on the table. This gentleman walks up and just kind of butted into the conversation while a bunch of us were there talking. And he said, "Hey, what's that?" I let him know that it was a new product that helps with stress. He said he had stress and wanted to try some of it.

I said, "Sure. Here's some to enjoy. It's a fun experience." And I handed him the energy drink. We're having a good time, right?

He said, "Wow! This is pretty good." He didn't leave. He just stayed there. Then, all of a sudden, he walked away and came back. He said, "Hey, can my friends over there try some of it?"

I said, "Absolutely! Let me pour you a few glasses of it." He took the glasses over to them. They tried it.

Pay It Forward works. Here's what happened. It was around lunch time. He said, "Hey, why don't we go up to my place? We'll grab a drink."

I looked at the group of around eight of us and said, "OK, why not?"

We get into the elevator and he pushes the "P" button. Now, I'm thinking it's one of two things, right? It's either the penthouse or the parking garage.

Well, the good news is that the elevator started going up. When we got to the top floor, the elevator opened up to the big penthouse at The Ritz Carlton, where, literally, was the owner's unit and was above the hotel. We walked into his unbelievably beautiful home that overlooked the entire city skyline of Miami. We were blown away.

You never know what can happen from those instant connections. As we were walking around his place, we started talking about the Superbowl. He said, "As a matter of fact, I do have two tickets for the game tonight."

I said, "You do?" He explained that he was not going to go.

I asked, "Is there any way that I can buy those tickets from you?" Because they were unbelievable seats.

He said, "No, you can't buy them from me. They're my gift to you." You see, when you believe in what's possible, everything becomes totally possible.

You've got to believe it and be genuine in your belief. You've got to live from that place of service. It doesn't mean live from the place of service once in a while. It means live from the place of service all the time.

In this situation, sure enough, what happened was we got great seats to the Superbowl. The principle of paying it forward works in every area of your life: it goes with your relationships; it goes with your business; and it goes with making a difference on the planet.

So, if you're having a challenging time in your business right now—maybe things aren't going exactly how you want them to go; maybe you're not having enough sales; or maybe you're not getting all the right connections— take a moment and say to yourself, "Maybe I'm just not doing it right." Then, find ways to "Pay It Forward."

I can only share with you that this process has worked over and over and over in many significant deals and programs and projects because I ask better questions about how to provide value first. You'll find that successful people ask better questions. They ask specific questions.

The big question to ask yourself today is, "What specifically can I do today to go out to the marketplace to create more value and help more people and expect nothing in return?"

By "Paying It Forward," the universe yields back. The bottom line is that when you "Pay It Forward," it works. You'll have more fun. You'll have more success. You'll truly come from that place of service. And when you come from an authentic place of service and help people, people can tell. Be inspired. Pray. Be authentic. Go out there and "Pay It Forward"—and live your dreams.

PART II

The Obvious Universal Laws for Business Success

The Obvious Law of Focus
The Obvious Law of Planning
The Obvious Law of Resource Management
The Obvious Law of Innovation & Change
The Obvious Law of Communication
The Obvious Law of Accountability
The Obvious Law of Productivity & Work Quality
The Obvious Law of Personal Character & Belief
The Obvious Law of Team Power
The Obvious Law of Negotiating
The Obvious Law of Mentorship & Practice
The Obvious Law of Service

About The Obvious Universal Laws for Business Success

These *Obvious* Laws point you in the right direction of what's important to focus on as you develop and maintain your business. Each of the Obvious Laws tell about an essential element, which is important as each one plays an individual part of your business *and* as each one works together with the other parts to help you achieve success. Some of them overlap more than others. For example, each of the Obvious Laws requires "Focus" for you to zero in on doing what's important to get the results related to that area.

The Obvious Laws target these areas:

- Focus
- Planning
- Resource Management
- Innovation & Change
- Communication
- Accountability
- Productivity & Work Quality
- Personal Character & Belief
- Team Power
- Negotiating
- Mentorship & Practice
- Service

Each one of the Obvious Laws has one thing in common: They all start with you!

It's important that you lead your business by setting a high standard in each area.

In Part III, each chapter first describes the Obvious Law focused on in that chapter. Then, it is followed by an assessment so you can reflect on how the one in focus currently impacts you, your business and the eleven other ones.

You can go back over these time and time again to get perspective on the current state of your business. Your answers in the assessment will change over time. I suggest you start a journal to record your answers at a given time and track your progress.

The specific details of how you put these laws into action may vary in some ways, depending upon your business. In the last part of this book, I mention how Powerteam International can show you even more about how to achieve business success.

3
The Obvious Law of Focus

The act of concentrating your time, energy and resources on achieving your vision.

[aka: "What do you call *'Ignore Distractions'*?"]

Interpretations & Applications of this Law include:

- Being able to focus starts with getting clear on your vision.

- Starting your vision with one goal and seeing where there are smaller goals that are part of it, will help you focus on different aspects of the big picture goal. Your vision may start out with one small goal and grow from there into the bigger vision, or it may start with an overall vision and be broken down into goals.

- Getting a clear focus is easy after developing your vision and your goals.

- Ignoring distractions that come up and take you away from your focus will help you stay focused rather than getting scattered.

- Without focusing, you will not know what to do and what not to do to get the results you want. So, get focused!

Assessment for *The Obvious Law of Focus*

Directions: *Consider <u>specifically</u> how The Obvious Law of Focus applies directly to your business. Answer the following questions on a regular basis to identify areas for improvement related to this Law. You may want to answer these questions on separate paper or on the computer as some of your answers will change over time.*

1. How does The Obvious Law of Focus apply to my business?

   _____

   _____

   _____

2. How does my effectiveness with this Law positively and/or negatively impact how the other Laws apply to my business?

The Obvious Law of Planning	
The Obvious Law of Resource Management	
The Obvious Law of Innovation & Change	
The Obvious Law of Communication	
The Obvious Law of Accountability	

The Obvious Law of *Productivity & Work Quality*	
The Obvious Law of *Personal Character & Belief*	
The Obvious Law of *Team Power*	
The Obvious Law of *Negotiating*	
The Obvious Law of *Mentorship & Practice*	
The Obvious Law of *Service*	

3. What do *I* specifically need to <u>stop doing today</u> and why?

    _____

    _____

    _____

4. What do *I* specifically need to <u>start doing today</u> and why?

    _____

    _____

    _____

5. What do *I* need to <u>continue doing</u> today and why?

_____

_____

_____

6. What does *my team* specifically need <u>to stop</u> doing and why?

_____

_____

_____

7. What does *my team* specifically need <u>to start</u> doing and why?

_____

_____

_____

8. What does *my team* specifically need <u>to continue</u> doing and why?

_____

_____

_____

9. What type of accountability and measure tracking systems need to exist?_____

_____

_____

10. How will the positive changes improve my business?

_____

_____

_____

Additional Thoughts:

_____

_____

_____

_____

_____

_____

_____

_____

_____

_____

_____

_____

_____

_____

_____

_____

_____

4
The Obvious Law of Planning

The act of determining upfront what actions are required and by when to achieve your vision.

[aka: "What do you call '*Think Ahead*'?"]

Interpretations & Applications of this Law include:

- Being able to plan starts with thinking ahead. Look at your end result – known as your vision - and then work back-wards. Ask yourself, "What action would give me that result?" Keep asking and answering that question and writing down the actions—until you get all the way back to the very first step you could possibly take from where you are now.

- Taking action from that very first step you identified—and then taking the next step and the next step will eventually move you towards getting results until you achieve your goal. (Sometimes the results are not overnight. So, be patient.)

- Making adjustments along the way as problems and chal-lenges come up will be necessary because you cannot antic-ipate everything. Keep your vision in mind and be consistently persistent so you stay focused.

- Without planning, you will not know what specific actions to take to achieve your vision. So, start planning!

Assessment for *The Obvious Law of Planning*

Directions: *Consider <u>specifically</u> how The Obvious Law of Planning applies directly to your business. Answer the following questions on a regular basis to identify areas for improvement related to this Law. You may want to answer these questions on separate paper or on the computer as some of your answers will change over time.*

1. How does The Obvious Law of Planning apply to my business?

    _____

    _____

    _____

2. How does my effectiveness with this Law positively and/or

    negatively impact how the other Laws apply to my business?

The Obvious Law of Focus	
The Obvious Law of Resource Management	
The Obvious Law of Innovation & Change	
The Obvious Law of Communication	
The Obvious Law of Accountability	

The Obvious Law of *Productivity & Work Quality*	
The Obvious Law of *Personal Character & Belief*	
The Obvious Law of *Team Power*	
The Obvious Law of *Negotiating*	
The Obvious Law of *Mentorship & Practice*	
The Obvious Law of *Service*	

3. What do *I* specifically need to <u>stop doing</u> and why?

_____

_____

_____

4. What do *I* specifically need to <u>start doing</u> and why?

_____

_____

_____

5. What do *I* need to <u>continue doing</u> and why?

    _____

    _____

    _____

6. What does *my team* specifically need <u>to stop</u> doing and why?

    _____

    _____

    _____

7. What does *my team* specifically need <u>to start</u> doing and why?

    _____

    _____

    _____

8. What does *my team* specifically need <u>to continue</u> doing and why?

    _____

    _____

    _____

9. What type of accountability and measure tracking systems need to exist?_____

    _____

    _____

10. How will the positive changes improve my business?

    _____

    _____

    _____

Additional Thoughts:

_____

_____

_____

_____

_____

_____

_____

_____

_____

_____

_____

_____

_____

_____

_____

5
The Obvious Law
of Resource Management

The act of identifying and managing the necessary resources to fulfill your vision.

[aka: *"What do you call 'Monitor Your Assets'?"*]

Interpretations & Applications of this Law include:

- Being able to manage your resources begins with seeing what resources you need to fulfill your vision and getting them.

- Recognizing that most resources needed are connected to money, time, people, energy and materials will help you identify the specific types needed.

- Prioritizing how many and how much is needed for each resource at each business development stage.

- Increasing your effectiveness in managing resources includes: (1) improving your Daily Mode of Operation (DMO), including 10 Before 10; (2) tracking and analyzing your measures; (3) tracking your money, including monetization, cost analysis, pricing strategies, and Profits & Losses.

- Without monitoring your resources and your assets, you may not be using them wisely. So, start taking inventory of your resources and then managing them well!

Assessment for *The Obvious Law of Resource Management*

Directions: *Consider specifically how The Obvious Law of Resource Management applies directly to your business. Answer the following questions on a regular basis to identify areas for improvement related to this Law. You may want to answer these questions on separate paper or on the computer as some of your answers will change over time.*

1. How does The Obvious Law of Resource Management apply to my business? _____

   _____

   _____

2. How does my effectiveness with this Law positively and/or negatively impact how the other Laws apply to my business?

The Obvious Law of Focus	
The Obvious Law of Planning	
The Obvious Law of Innovation & Change	
The Obvious Law of Communication	

The Obvious Law of Accountability	
The Obvious Law of Productivity & Work Quality	
The Obvious Law of Personal Character & Belief	
The Obvious Law of Team Power	
The Obvious Law of Negotiating	
The Obvious Law of Mentorship & Practice	
The Obvious Law of Service	

3. What do *I* specifically need to <u>stop doing</u> and why?

   _____

   _____

   _____

4. What do *I* specifically need to <u>start doing</u> and why?

   _____

   _____

   _____

5. What do *I* need to <u>continue doing</u> and why?

_____

_____

_____

6. What does *my team* specifically need <u>to stop</u> doing and why?

_____

_____

_____

7. What does *my team* specifically need <u>to start</u> doing and why?

_____

_____

_____

8. What does *my team* specifically need <u>to continue</u> doing and why?

_____

_____

_____

9. What type of accountability and measure tracking systems need to exist?_____

_____

_____

10. How will the positive changes improve my business?

_____

_____

_____

Additional Thoughts:

6
The Obvious Law
of Innovation & Change

The act of creating new aspects of your business to stay competitive.

[aka: "What do you call '*Avoid the Status Quo*'?"]

Interpretations & Applications of this Law include:

- Being able to adapt and change with the times and being innovative are key to lasting success.

- Creating innovative changes in your products, services and/or business structure is inevitable. However, there are some things that will stay the same no matter what, such as having a commitment to providing high quality innovations.

- Recognizing market trends and problems to solve based on information available within your business and outside of your business will help you see what changes to make in keeping your business on the cutting edge.

- Having cutting-edge marketing and timing is closely tied to being seen in the marketplace as innovative and changing with the market.

- Being pragmatic and visionary in innovative marketing that brands and manages the image of how that brand is presented is important.

- Without innovating and changing, you may get stuck being status quo and then become obsolete. So, start finding what to change and how!

Assessment for *The Obvious Law of Innovation & Change*

Directions: *Consider <u>specifically</u> how The Obvious Law of Innovation & Change applies directly to your business. Answer the following questions on a regular basis to identify areas for improvement related to this Law. You may want to answer these questions on separate paper or on the computer as some of your answers will change over time.*

1. How does The Obvious Law of Innovation & Change apply to my business? _____

    _____

    _____

2. How does my effectiveness with this Law positively and/or negatively impact how the other Laws apply to my business?

The Obvious Law of Focus	
The Obvious Law of Planning	
The Obvious Law of Resource Management	
The Obvious Law of Communication	

The Obvious Law of Accountability	
The Obvious Law of Productivity & Work Quality	
The Obvious Law of Personal Character & Belief	
The Obvious Law of Team Power	
The Obvious Law of Negotiating	
The Obvious Law of Mentorship & Practice	
The Obvious Law of Service	

3. What do *I* specifically need to <u>stop doing</u> and why?

_____

_____

_____

4. What do *I* specifically need to <u>start doing</u> and why?

_____

_____

_____

5. What do *I* need to <u>continue doing</u> and why?

    _____

    _____

    _____

6. What does *my team* specifically need <u>to stop</u> doing and why?

    _____

    _____

    _____

7. What does *my team* specifically need <u>to start</u> doing and why?

    _____

    _____

    _____

8. What does *my team* specifically need <u>to continue</u> doing and why?

    _____

    _____

    _____

9. What type of accountability and measure tracking systems need to exist?_____

    _____

    _____

10. How will the positive changes improve my business?

    _____

    _____

    _____

Additional Thoughts:

7
The Obvious Law
of Communication

The act of conveying information in an inspiring and effective manner towards a common understanding so everyone works to fulfill the vision.

[aka: "What do you call 'Share Your Vision'?"]

Interpretations & Applications of this Law include:

- Being able to communicate effectively starts with looking at how you share your vision. First, be sure your vision inspires others. Then, share that vision in an inspiring way.

- Knowing what to communicate is important. Not all communication is about your vision directly, but it often is connected somehow.

- Communicating powerfully and positively with others starts with how you communicate with yourself on the inside, starting with your beliefs and your inspiration. You set the standard for communication both within your business and between your business and others.

- Identifying who to communicate with and how often is important and it impacts the results you get. Regularly communicate with your team, network and growing customer base to increase your lasting success.

- Without effectively communicating, you will not be able to listen and respond to the market. So, keep communicating!

Assessment for *The Obvious Law of Communication*

Directions: *Consider <u>specifically</u> how The Obvious Law of Communication applies directly to your business. Answer the following questions on a regular basis to identify areas for improvement related to this Law. You may want to answer these questions on separate paper or on the computer as some of your answers will change over time.*

1. How does The Obvious Law of Communication apply to my business?

   _____

   _____

   _____

2. How does my effectiveness with this Law positively and/or negatively impact how the other Laws apply to my business?

The Obvious Law of *Focus*	
The Obvious Law of *Planning*	
The Obvious Law of *Resource Management*	
The Obvious Law of *Innovation & Change*	

The Obvious Law of *Accountability*	
The Obvious Law of *Productivity & Work Quali-*	
The Obvious Law of *Personal Character & Belief*	
The Obvious Law of *Team Power*	
The Obvious Law of *Negotiating*	
The Obvious Law of *Mentorship & Practice*	
The Obvious Law of *Service*	

3. What do *I* specifically need to <u>stop doing</u> and why?

    _____

    _____

    _____

4. What do *I* specifically need to <u>start doing</u> and why?

    _____

    _____

    _____

5. What do *I* need to <u>continue doing</u> and why?

    _____

    _____

    _____

6. What does *my team* specifically need <u>to stop</u> doing and why?

    _____

    _____

    _____

7. What does *my team* specifically need <u>to start</u> doing and why?

    _____

    _____

    _____

8. What does *my team* specifically need <u>to continue</u> doing and why?

    _____

    _____

    _____

9. What type of accountability and measure tracking systems need to exist?_____

    _____

    _____

10. How will the positive changes improve my business?

    _____

    _____

    _____

Additional Thoughts:

_____

_____

_____

_____

_____

_____

_____

_____

_____

_____

_____

_____

_____

_____

_____

8
The Obvious Law
of Accountability

The act of delivering on your commitments.

[aka: "What do you call '*Follow Through*'?"]

Interpretations & Applications of this Law include:

- Being able to be accountable and follow through is key to being successful.

- Identifying who is accountable for what is important. Accountability is important to every aspect of your business.

- Remembering that the power of accountability starts with you will help you recognize how important it is to lead by example.

- Knowing what strengths everyone on your team has will help you know who to delegate certain tasks to so that your team each contributes. Then, recognize them for what they each do.

- Working together to achieve the tasks necessary to make the vision happen also involves mundane tasks. Help your team link them with the big picture vision to see how important details are in getting things done.

- Without accountability, you and your team will not be able to accomplish what it takes to achieve your vision. So, get accountable!

Assessment for *The Obvious Law of Accountability*

Directions: *Consider <u>specifically</u> how The Obvious Law of Accountability applies directly to your business. Answer the following questions on a regular basis to identify areas for improvement related to this Law. You may want to answer these questions on separate paper or on the computer as some of your answers will change over time.*

1. How does The Obvious Law of Accountability apply to my business?

   _____

   _____

   _____

2. How does my effectiveness with this Law positively and/or negatively impact how the other Laws apply to my business?

The Obvious Law of *Focus*	
The Obvious Law of *Planning*	
The Obvious Law of *Resource Management*	
The Obvious Law of *Innovation & Change*	

The Obvious Law of Communication	
The Obvious Law of Productivity & Work Quality	
The Obvious Law of Personal Character & Belief	
The Obvious Law of Team Power	
The Obvious Law of Negotiating	
The Obvious Law of Mentorship & Practice	
The Obvious Law of Service	

3. What do *I* specifically need to <u>stop doing</u> and why?

_____

_____

_____

4. What do *I* specifically need to <u>start doing</u> and why?

_____

_____

_____

5. What do *I* need to <u>continue doing</u> and why?

_____

_____

_____

6. What does *my team* specifically need <u>to stop</u> doing and why?

_____

_____

_____

7. What does *my team* specifically need <u>to start</u> doing and why?

_____

_____

_____

8. What does *my team* specifically need <u>to continue</u> doing and why?

_____

_____

_____

9. What type of accountability and measure tracking systems need to exist?_____

_____

_____

10. How will the positive changes improve my business?

_____

_____

_____

Additional Thoughts:

_____

_____

_____

_____

_____

_____

_____

_____

_____

_____

_____

_____

_____

_____

_____

_____

9
The Obvious Law
of Productivity & Work Quality

The act of working effectively to consistently get quality results.

[aka: "What do you call *'Take Pride in Your Results'*?"]

Interpretations & Applications of this Law include:

- Being able to be productive and do quality work starts with knowing what to do and knowing what the standard is for producing quality work.

- Taking pride in what you produce allows you to persevere through the mundane tasks it takes to produce the results you want.

- Creating systems allows you to increase your productivity and consistency in doing quality work. There needs to be an overall work system with smaller work systems within the bigger picture.

- Relating your systems to your daily operations, your measures, and your data and trend analysis helps you know how you are doing.

- Producing quality work relates to quality products and services—and anything else that goes into producing the end results.

- Without producing quality work consistently, you will not get be able to create lasting success. So, get productive using high quality work standards!

Assessment for *The Obvious Law of Productivity & Work Quality*

Directions: *Consider <u>specifically</u> how The Obvious Law of Productivity & Work Quality applies directly to your business. Answer the following questions on a regular basis to identify areas for improvement related to this Law. You may want to answer these questions on separate paper or on the computer as some of your answers will change over time.*

1. How does The Obvious Law of Productivity & Work Quality apply to my business? _____

   _____

   _____

2. How does my effectiveness with this Law positively and/or negatively impact how the other Laws apply to my business?

The Obvious Law of Focus	
The Obvious Law of Planning	
The Obvious Law of Resource Management	

The Obvious Law of *Innovation & Change*	
The Obvious Law of *Communication*	
The Obvious Law of *Accountability*	
The Obvious Law of *Personal Character & Belief*	
The Obvious Law of *Team Power*	
The Obvious Law of *Negotiating*	
The Obvious Law of *Mentorship & Practice*	
The Obvious Law of *Service*	

3. What do *I* specifically need to <u>stop doing</u> and why?

_____

_____

_____

4. What do *I* specifically need to <u>start doing</u> and why?

_____

_____

_____

5. What do *I* need to <u>continue doing</u> and why?

_____

_____

_____

6. What does *my team* specifically need <u>to stop</u> doing and why?

_____

_____

_____

7. What does *my team* specifically need <u>to start</u> doing and why?

_____

_____

_____

8. What does *my team* specifically need <u>to continue</u> doing and why?

_____

_____

_____

9. What type of accountability and measure tracking systems need to exist?

_____

_____

_____

10. How will the positive changes improve my business?

_____

_____

_____

Additional Thoughts:

_____

_____

_____

_____

_____

_____

_____

_____

_____

_____

_____

_____

10
The Obvious Law
of Personal Character & Belief

The act of having the discipline to do the right thing, despite your circumstances.

[aka: "What do you call '*Become Strong on The Inside*'?"]

Interpretations & Applications of this Law include:

- Having the belief in yourself and your abilities to achieve your dream is important. Keeping your why alive drives your actions.

- Maintaining your commitments to do what you need to do with unwavering integrity and ethics helps you build a solid foundation.

- Managing your emotions keeps you from letting them lead your actions, especially self-centeredness and fear that may keep you from being able to come from an authentic place of service.

- Developing the strength to achieve is important. There are many ways that you will be challenged. As you improve your skills and abilities as well as strengthen your character, it becomes easier to achieve.

- Having the discipline and perseverance to do what you need to do will increase your ability to perform and achieve.

- Without personal character, you may undermine your own success. So, develop positive personal characteristics that last!

Assessment for *The Obvious Law of Personal Character & Belief*

Directions: *Consider <u>specifically</u> how The Obvious Law of Personal Character & Belief applies directly to your business. Answer the following questions on a regular basis to identify areas for improvement related to this Law. You may want to answer these questions on separate paper or on the computer as some of your answers will change over time.*

1. How does The Obvious Law of Personal Character & Belief apply to my business? _____

    _____

    _____

2. How does my effectiveness with this Law positively and/or negatively impact how the other Laws apply to my business?

The Obvious Law of Focus	
The Obvious Law of Planning	

The Obvious Law of *Resource Management*	
The Obvious Law of *Innovation & Change*	
The Obvious Law of *Communication*	
The Obvious Law of *Accountability*	
The Obvious Law of *Productivity & Work Quality*	
The Obvious Law of *Team Power*	
The Obvious Law of *Negotiating*	
The Obvious Law of *Mentorship & Practice*	
The Obvious Law of *Service*	

3. What do *I* specifically need to <u>stop doing</u> and why?

   _____

   _____

   _____

4. What do *I* specifically need to <u>start doing</u> and why?

_____

_____

_____

5. What do *I* need to <u>continue doing</u> and why?

_____

_____

_____

6. What does *my team* specifically need <u>to stop</u> doing and why?

_____

_____

_____

7. What does *my team* specifically need <u>to start</u> doing and why?

_____

_____

_____

8. What does *my team* specifically need <u>to continue</u> doing and why?

_____

_____

_____

9. What type of accountability and measure tracking systems need to exist?_____

_____

_____

10. How will the positive changes improve my business?

_____

_____

_____

Additional Thoughts:

_____

_____

_____

_____

_____

_____

_____

_____

_____

_____

_____

_____

_____

11
The Obvious Law of Team Power

The act of working together to achieve a common vision.

[aka: "What do you call '*Find People Inspired to Win with You*'?"]

Interpretations & Applications of this Law include:

- Building an effective team of experts committed to your vision will help you win.

- Reaching out to build a network of partners includes working with your Mastermind Teams (the one pulling you up and the one you're pulling up), others in your network, and your customers.

- Having different types of teamwork involved in getting things done means that you may have a core team and extended network of partners. You can delegate responsibilities to your team to share the workload, specifically based on knowledge and skills expertise.

- Valuing the work your team does increases the inspiration and performance they do—and there will be more fun in the process!

- Without teaming up with a well-chosen team, it is much more difficult to achieve your vision. So, build your team and your network!

Assessment for *The Obvious Law of Team Power*

Directions: *Consider <u>specifically</u> how The Obvious Law of Team Power applies directly to your business. Answer the following questions on a regular basis to identify areas for improvement related to this Law. You may want to answer these questions on separate paper or on the computer as some of your answers will change over time.*

1. How does The Obvious Law of Team Power apply to my business?

    _____

    _____

    _____

2. How does my effectiveness with this Law positively and/or negatively impact how the other Laws apply to my business?

The Obvious Law of Focus	
The Obvious Law of Planning	
The Obvious Law of Resource Management	
The Obvious Law of Innovation & Change	
The Obvious Law of Communication	

The Obvious Law of *Accountability*	
The Obvious Law of *Productivity & Work Quality*	
The Obvious Law of *Personal Character & Belief*	
The Obvious Law of *Negotiating*	
The Obvious Law of *Mentorship & Practice*	
The Obvious Law of *Service*	

3. What do *I* specifically need to <u>stop doing</u> and why?

_____

_____

_____

4. What do *I* specifically need to <u>start doing</u> and why?

_____

_____

_____

5. What do *I* need to <u>continue doing</u> and why?

_____

_____

_____

6. What does *my team* specifically need <u>to stop</u> doing and why?

_____

_____

_____

7. What does *my team* specifically need <u>to start</u> doing and why?

_____

_____

_____

8. What does *my team* specifically need <u>to continue</u> doing and why?

_____

_____

_____

9. What type of accountability and measure tracking systems need to exist?_____

_____

_____

10. How will the positive changes improve my business?

_____

_____

_____

Additional Thoughts:

_____

_____

_____

_____

_____

_____

_____

_____

_____

_____

_____

_____

_____

_____

_____

_____

_____

_____

12
The Obvious Law of Negotiating

The act of establishing a mutually beneficial agreement for exchanging value between two or more parties.

[aka: "What do you call '*Make the Agreement a Win-Win*'?"]

Interpretations & Applications of this Law include:

- Buying and/or selling products and/or services so it benefits those involved in the exchange is fundamental to business. Products and services may include a variety of aspects involving time, money, materials, network connections, etc.

- Having a written contract is a good practice so that it clearly states what the agreement is between parties. There are different legal considerations for different areas. So, have qualified attorneys review the agreements you make before the final agreement.

- Identifying which partnerships to have is important so you negotiate with people who will be fair in the agreement. Some negotiations may be short-term and others ongoing. It is a good practice to have an end date and time for the current contract so you can renegotiate.

- Without negotiating effectively, some partnerships may not work. So start negotiating well!

Assessment for *The Obvious Law of Negotiating*

Directions: *Consider <u>specifically</u> how The Obvious Law of Negotiating applies directly to your business. Answer the following questions on a regular basis to identify areas for improvement related to this Law. You may want to answer these questions on separate paper or on the computer as some of your answers will change over time.*

1. How does The Obvious Law of Negotiating apply to my business?

    _____

    _____

    _____

2. How does my effectiveness with this Law positively and/or

    negatively impact how the other Laws apply to my business?

The Obvious Law of Focus	
The Obvious Law of Planning	
The Obvious Law of Resource Management	
The Obvious Law of Innovation & Change	
The Obvious Law of Communication	

The Obvious Law of Accountability	
The Obvious Law of Productivity & Work Quali-ty	
The Obvious Law of Personal Character & Belief	
The Obvious Law of Team Power	
The Obvious Law of Mentorship & Practice	
The Obvious Law of Service	

3. What do *I* specifically need to <u>stop doing</u> and why?

_____

_____

_____

4. What do *I* specifically need to <u>start doing</u> and why?

_____

_____

_____

5. What do *I* need to <u>continue doing</u> and why?

    _____

    _____

    _____

6. What does *my team* specifically need <u>to stop</u> doing and why?

    _____

    _____

    _____

7. What does *my team* specifically need <u>to start</u> doing and why?

    _____

    _____

    _____

8. What does *my team* specifically need <u>to continue</u> doing and why?

    _____

    _____

    _____

9. What type of accountability and measure tracking systems need to exist?_____

    _____

    _____

10. How will the positive changes improve my business?

    _____

    _____

    _____

Additional Thoughts:

13
The Obvious Law
of Mentorship & Practice

The act of learning from others who have already achieved the success you seek and then passing it on to others.

[aka: "What do you call '*Learn From Others and Apply*'?"]

Interpretations & Applications of this Law include:

- Being mentored and mentoring others should be an ongoing process, where you have two Mastermind Teams (where one pulls you up and you pull the other up). It keeps you in the process of connecting, learning, growing and serving so you continue to improve and stay on the cutting edge in your business as you develop your skills.

- Knowing and specializing in a certain area of expertise is important. However, it is also important to know about certain business skills.

- Learning from and being open to other people's feedback about their mistakes and failures can help you reduce yours.

- Receiving mentorship may mean you directly or indirectly learn from them or you may need to invest in your education—or both.

- Without giving and receiving mentorship, your practices may not be as sharp as needed to succeed more rapidly. Find quality mentors to work with and start practicing what works!

Assessment for *The Obvious Law of Mentorship & Practice*

Directions: *Consider <u>specifically</u> how The Obvious Law of Mentorship & Practice applies directly to your business. Answer the following questions on a regular basis to identify areas for improvement related to this Law. You may want to answer these questions on separate paper or on the computer as some of your answers will change over time.*

1. How does The Obvious Law of Mentorship & Practice apply to my business? _____

   _____

   _____

2. How does my effectiveness with this Law positively and/or negatively impact how the other Laws apply to my business?

The Obvious Law of *Focus*	
The Obvious Law of *Planning*	
The Obvious Law of *Resource Management*	
The Obvious Law of *Innovation & Change*	

The Obvious Law of *Communication*	
The Obvious Law of *Accountability*	
The Obvious Law of *Productivity & Work Quality*	
The Obvious Law of *Personal Character & Belief*	
The Obvious Law of *Team Power*	
The Obvious Law of *Negotiating*	
The Obvious Law of *Service*	

3. What do *I* specifically need to <u>stop doing</u> and why?

———————————————————————————————

———————————————————————————————

———————————————————————————————

4. What do *I* specifically need to <u>start doing</u> and why?

———————————————————————————————

———————————————————————————————

———————————————————————————————

5. What do *I* need to <u>continue doing</u> and why?

    _____

    _____

    _____

6. What does *my team* specifically need <u>to stop</u> doing and why?

    _____

    _____

    _____

7. What does *my team* specifically need <u>to start</u> doing and why?

    _____

    _____

    _____

8. What does *my team* specifically need <u>to continue</u> doing and why?

    _____

    _____

    _____

9. What type of accountability and measure tracking systems need to exist?_____

    _____

    _____

10. How will the positive changes improve my business?

    _____

    _____

    _____

Additional Thoughts:

_____

_____

_____

_____

_____

_____

_____

_____

_____

_____

_____

_____

_____

_____

_____

14
The Obvious Law of Service

The act of finding ways to build relationships and contribute to other people's lives in addition to fulfilling your own needs.

[aka: "What do you call *'Give First without Expecting Anything Back'*?"]

Interpretations & Applications of this Law include:

- Giving and Receiving is a natural occurrence, but sometimes we block one or the other. The more you give, the more you receive. If you give freely of your time, energy and resources, it comes back to you directly and indirectly.

- Leading with the motto captured in the common saying "What's in it for me?" makes it difficult to serve. Instead ask, "What's in it for <u>them</u>?" It is based on the "Pay It Forward" concept and practice.

- Serving others is similar, whether it is serving others who are partners, team members or customers. However, the way you serve may look different depending upon your relationship with them. Coming from a true place of genuine service, though, gives you the ability to be consistent.

- Making quality service a hallmark of your business practice that runs throughout your entire business will give you the competitive advantage to win.

- Without serving others authentically, your business will not thrive as it could. So, start serving with enthusiasm to make a true difference!

Assessment for The *Obvious Law of Service*

Directions: *Consider <u>specifically</u> how The Obvious Law of Service applies directly to your business. Answer the following questions on a regular basis to identify areas for improvement related to this Law. You may want to answer these questions on separate paper or on the computer as some of your answers will change over time.*

1. How does The Obvious Law of Service apply to my business?

    _____

    _____

    _____

2. How does my effectiveness with this Law positively and/or negatively impact how the other Laws apply to my business?

The Obvious Law of Focus	
The Obvious Law of Planning	
The Obvious Law of Resource Management	
The Obvious Law of Innovation & Change	

The Obvious Law of Communication	
The Obvious Law of Accountability	
The Obvious Law of Productivity & Work Quality	
The Obvious Law of Personal Character & Belief	
The Obvious Law of Team Power	
The Obvious Law of Negotiating	
The Obvious Law of Mentorship & Practice	

3. What do *I* specifically need to <u>stop doing</u> and why?

_____

_____

_____

4. What do *I* specifically need to <u>start doing</u> and why?

_____

_____

_____

5. What do *I* need to <u>continue doing</u> and why?

_____

_____

_____

6. What does *my team* specifically need <u>to stop</u> doing and why?

_____

_____

_____

7. What does *my team* specifically need <u>to start</u> doing and why?

_____

_____

_____

8. What does *my team* specifically need <u>to continue</u> doing and why?

_____

_____

_____

9. What type of accountability and measure tracking systems need to exist?_____

_____

_____

10. How will the positive changes improve my business?

_____

_____

_____

Additional Thoughts:

_____

_____

_____

_____

_____

_____

_____

_____

_____

_____

_____

_____

_____

_____

_____

PART III

The Obvious
Universal Laws in Action

15
Live the Dream

Have you ever thought about living that perfect dream? What does that look like? Let me tell you where it all starts. It all starts with you. If you want to have more success and if you want to have all the things that people talk about, you've got to start with the inside success first.

What are you doing to live that dream? Maybe you've seen a dream vacation spot you think would be nice to visit or would be a perfect place to live. How does it happen that you get to visit or live there? You always hear about people who have lots of success and live the dream. But what did they have to do to get there to enjoy all the benefits?

You see, that's the secret. They don't tell you that it takes hard work. The hard work is actually part of the Obvious that it takes to be successful, which is what this book describes.

As I mentioned earlier, Gary Player says, "The luckiest people out there tend to work the hardest." Think about it for yourself. How do you create more success? How do you live that dream? I can tell you that by studying so many successful companies and studying failures as well, there are some common ingredients.

But I can tell you that the No. 1 ingredient that you have to invest in is your education. Some of that education will be to work on you; and some of that education will be to work on business. They're connected, though, because you are the driver of your business. Because business environments change, you need to stay ahead by the things you do to educate yourself. You cannot control everything about your business internally or externally, but the more you know, the easier it is to make wise decisions and be a positive influence that impacts your success.

You've got to have total faith and belief in what's possible. When there's absolute faith, there's no room for fear. Are you looking for things to get better? Do you want to live that amazing dream you always hear about? It starts with you. It starts with understanding that if you want things to change, you've got to change. If you want things to get better, you've got to get better. You see, you're taking the first step by reading this book. It'll help you understand how I really do all of those things, how I create success even when I have so many distractions.

Write this one down: all distractions are equal. That's right, all distractions are equal. So, start asking yourself if you're doing the right actions every day to have that success. You will increase your awareness of just being busy or really being productive. Being busy and being productive are two very different things. As I study successful people, I see lots of people who are super busy, but they aren't getting ahead.

Did you ever notice there are people around you who are not as smart as you who have had a lot more success? Why is that? I would much rather focus on and work with ignorance on fire than have knowledge on ice.

Start to think about your own life. What's working? What's not working? You may even have some mixture of areas that are sort of working, meaning they're really not working the way you want.

So, where does it all start to get things working? It starts with having the inside emotions, the inside beliefs, and the inside faith. You see, with absolute faith, there's no room for fear. If you don't like where things are right now, take a really good look at things on the inside. If you're sick and tired of being sick and tired and are ready for a change, what it takes is understanding.

How do I get around the right people? How do I get the right education? How do I learn the skills to allow my brain to think differently? You're destined for greatness. It's only the inside that holds you back. Your mental programs.

The programs are continuously engrained. As a kid, we're told "No" over and over and over and over and over. So, what do you think gets engrained? As I said earlier, if you watch the news, it's not positive. You know it's negative. So, if you wake up to negative and go to bed to negative you become really negative.

You see, when you listen to the audio CDs in our *Success by Design* program and watch the videos, it's going to help you understand how to develop success on the inside first – and then live it on the outside.

Get your posture and your belief system in the right place first. Then, you're ready for the next part of having the right systems. The systems will help you have the right ability to connect with people. You need to have both an online presence that works and an offline daily method of operation that works. Both will allow you to be more effective and make more money.

Have you ever asked the question, "How do I make more money?" That's always the question, right? You may want more money because you want this or that. No, you don't want more money. What you truly want is the wisdom to create more value so that more money just flows towards you—just like the waves flowing toward the sand on the shore. It happens automatically.

You see, when you create so much value in the marketplace, the money will come at you. And if you're serious about making changes in your life, if you're ready for the big programs, you've got to get started.

Invest in the education. Buy the programs that you know other people are using that works. When you begin to use our Success by Design System, it will lay out the tracks for you.

How do you have the best plan to win? How do you begin to think about specific answers to these questions: "Where am I going? How will I get there? Who will I get there with?"

Could you imagine owning your goals? Could you imagine having the power inside you to achieve? Could you imagine knowing the processes that it takes to live those dreams?

That's what we do at Powerteam International. Since we designed our own program, it's specifically designed to help you understand the language that commands you to win.

Once you've done all that, both the mindset and the posture are right for success. Then, get some of the systems on track and put them in motion. Next you've got to be with the right people. Think about who is on your mastermind team. If you're inspired and you're educated—you're going to win. What if you could be around people on a day in and day out basis who are cheering for you?

Often in your life you will find yourself surrounded by really negative people, who just want to keep you down. They want you to stay exactly where you are at. If you're ready for a big change and are looking for a huge increase—maybe it's changing your zip code, maybe it's a new car, maybe it's giving back to your kids, or whatever is most important for you—you've got to have the belief system. You've got to have the systems. You have to get the right teams around you.

When you do the Obvious, you get to live the dream life you design!

16
Powerteam International

I built Powerteam International to create more value that makes a difference in business and in the world. As I mentioned at the beginning of this book, my vision in creating Powerteam in 1996 started by my drive to empower others to live their business and lifestyle dreams.

We have programs and events to provide you and your business with what it takes to succeed in today's business world. Through our programs, you will find the right combination of business coaching, integrated learning programs, motivational workshops and personal development training to fit your needs.

Doing the Obvious and achieving business success does not have to wait until one of our events, though. The great news is that you can *start now*!

When you order our *Success by Design* program, it's going to change your life. The information in the audio series, DVDs and workbooks is all inclusive to help you get on the right track to create all the success you want and deserve.

I'm so excited about your future! I look forward to meeting you at one of our upcoming Powerteam International events. You can contact the person who told you about Powerteam International – or – just visit our website www.obviousglobal.com and you'll find all the information.

The key today is to *just get started*. It's your future. Our team's focus is to provide you with the power, tools, resources and connections for you to make your future bright—starting now!

17
Take Action Now

If you could put all that in one place so that you have the right education, the right team, and the right systems...then, you become unstoppable. If you're ready to become unstoppable, it all starts with you.

Our *Success by Design* system is designed to give you the "how to get inspired" versus the "how to be motivated." It also shows you how to connect with millionaires. If you'd like to start changing the way you think, and then bringing more of that stuff into your life, take action.

I know you're ready for it. Nobody is set up to be average. You're destined to be great, but you have to start with the idea that you're ready <u>now</u>. You're ready to take action. You're ready to learn the new processes.

We live in a new age. You have to understand the power of the web and how it works. More importantly, though, you have to have some fun with it. Think about how you can create more value for others.

It may be tough at first to know how to create more value for others who may have more success than you because you may not be exactly sure how to get through the processes to get the end result. But, if you're totally serious about taking life to the next level, I know you're ready for it.

I've worked with great people like Brian Tracy, Mark Victor Hanson, and Les Brown by helping them change their businesses. I actively look for ways to help a lot of these guys change their businesses because the thought process we have is about how we can help tens of thousands, even millions, of people by giving out a great message.

If you're ready for that, I would love to learn more about what you're trying to do and help you do that.

To your continued Success,

Bill Walsh

About the Author

Bill Walsh

*Business Coach / Venture Capitalist /
Entrepreneur / Movie Star / Speaker / Author*

Bill Walsh is President/CEO of Powerteam International that provides top quality coaching through its programs. One common theme that runs throughout Bill's many roles as a Business Coach, Venture Capitalist, Entrepreneur, Movie Star, Speaker and Author is that he is driven to make a lasting difference in life by empowering others to find success and live their dreams. Bill was featured in the movie *Pass It On.* He truly lives the message of creating massive value for others in all of his endeavors. He has three wonderful children—Austin, Marissa and Evan—who all live in the greater Chicago area. You can contact Bill and his team at Powerteam International 866-238-5920.

Special Bonus Offer

Go to www.obviousglobal.com to take advantage of over $1,000 in complimentary Bonuses including tickets to upcoming events, videos and other resources that I personally want to give you to help you start growing your business. So take action now!